The Provinces & Cities of CHINA

Lynn M. Stone

The Rourke Book Company, Inc.
Vero Beach, Florida 32964

© 2001 The Rourke Book Company, Inc.

PHOTO CREDITS
All Photos © Keren Su

Library of Congress Cataloging-in-Publication Data

Stone, Lynn M.
  The provinces & cities of China / Lynn M. Stone.
    p. cm. — (China)
  Includes index.
  ISBN 1-55916-320-8
  1. China—Juvenile literature. [1. China] I. Title: Provinces & cities of China.
II. Title

DS706 .S7952 2000
951—dc21
                                           00–039006

Printed in the USA

CONTENTS

CHINA DIVIDED

China is a huge country. Like the United States, China is divided into smaller areas. The U.S. calls its largest areas states. A large part of China is divided into units called provinces. Within the provinces are counties, villages, and cities.

In addition, China has several "**independent regions.**" Each of these five regions has its own special identity.

China's huge population, over 1 billion, lives mainly in the provinces of eastern China.

INDEPENDENT REGIONS

"Independent" means free to choose. In fact, China's independent regions are only partly independent. Like the provinces, the independent regions are part of the nation as a whole.

China's independent regions are Manchuria, Tibet, Turkestan, Xingiang, and Inner Mongolia. Each region is home to one or more **minority** groups.

Tibetan girls hold their lambs in Shigatse in the independent region of Tibet.

Minorities are groups which make up small parts of the whole. Most people in China, more than 9 of every 10, belong to the Han group. The Han are, by far, China's **majority** people. Native Tibetan people, for example, make up just a minority of the people in China. But the Tibetans have their own language and culture, different from the Han. Each of the independent regions has a certain amount of freedom to keep its own language and culture.

Aboard a camel, a sheepherder watches his flock in the Taklimakan Desert of Xinjiang.

玉磨坊
卡拉
OK
娛樂
NIGHT CLUB

金爵夜總會
NIGHT CLUB

中華

胡芬妮美容中心
美國嘉寶娜國際美容學校
CA BOTANA INT'L ACADEMY OF AESTHETICS
彌敦大廈 5/F 1座

HONG KONG

Another special part of China is Hong Kong. Hong Kong was ruled by England for many years. It was returned to Chinese rule in 1997.

Hong Kong is made up largely of Chinese Han people. But, for now, Hong Kong is free to carry on **commerce** – buying and selling – as if it were a British or American city. Elsewhere in China, commerce is far more controlled by the central Chinese government.

Traffic wheels along Nathan Road in Kowloon, the commerce center of Hong Kong.

*A Sani woman carries rice straw in Yunnan Province,
home to 24 minority groups.*

*A fisherman poles along the Li River in scenic Yangshuo,
Guangxi Province.*

SPECIAL CITY DISTRICTS

China also has four "special city districts." Each has a government apart from the government of the province.

China's special city districts are Shanghai, Beijing, Chongqing, and Tianjin. Each district includes the city itself and the suburbs around it.

Shanghai is China's largest city. It has a **population** of more than 8 million. Shanghai is a leading **port**. As China's top-ranking industrial city it is a world leader in commerce.

A caravan of boats called "junks" motor along the waterfront of Shanhai.

Beijing is China's second-largest city. It is the nation's capital and **cultural** center. Beijing has beautiful palaces, temples, and art treasures. The city is the seat of China's powerful central government.

Chongqing is an island city on the Yangtze River. Chongqing's history dates back 4,000 years, to the early days of China's ancient civilization.

Tianjin is a major trading center and a river port for Beijing, which is 85 miles (136 kilometers) northwest.

The Forbidden City of Beijing is one of China's cultural treasures.

CITIES AND PROVINCES

Many Chinese cities are a blend of the new, modern China and the old China. Thousands of bicycles share roadways with growing numbers of cars. Big department stores and flashy hotels stand near open, streetside markets and shops.

Many Chinese cities and provinces are famous for their food, culture, history, or beauty. Kunming in southwest China's Yunnan Province is the "City of Eternal Spring." Kunming is known for its pleasant weather!

The sun sets over West Lake in Hangzhou, Zhejing Province.

Much of Yunnan and nearby Guizhou Province have grand scenery. And Yunnan has 24 different minority groups.

Hangzhou is a city of parks, gardens, and rich history in Zhejiang Province. Suzhou is another city of gardens, and a city of canals and stone bridges.

The city of Wuxi lies along China's Grand Canal, built 1,400 years ago. Its gardens and Lake Taihu in Jiangsu Province draw thousands of visitors.

One of China's most remarkable cities is Lhasa. It rests in the mountains of Tibet, 12,000 feet (3,658 meters) above sea level!

Junks line the Grand Canal in Jiangsu Province.

Guilin in Guangxi Province is well-known for its beautiful mountains and river scenery.

Sichuan Province is well-known for its spicy food. But many Chinese believe the best food in China is in Guandong Province.

GLOSSARY

commerce (KAH MERS) — the exchange or buying and selling of items which involves transportation

cultural (KULCH rul) — having to do with a group's culture, its special ways of living

independent (IN duh PEN dent) — free to make choices; acting on one's own without help

majority (muh JAWR uh tee) — the largest group; more than half

minority (muh NAWR uh tee) — a small group within a much larger one

population (pah pyoo LAY shun) — the total number of people living in a place

port (PAWRT) — a seaside city where ships load and unload goods

FURTHER INFORMATION

Find out more about China's provinces and China in general with these helpful books and information sites:

- Baldwin, Robert F. *Daily Life in Ancient and Modern Beijing.* Lerner, 1999
- Finney, Susan and Kindle, Patricia. *China Then and Now.* Schaffer Publications, 1996
- Kent, Deborah. *Beijing.* Children's Press, 1996
- Steele, Phillip. *Step into the Chinese Empire.* Anness, 1998
- Stewart, Whitney. *The 14th Dalai Lama: Spiritual Leader of Tibet.* Lerner, 1996

China on-line at www.mytravelguide.com
Lonely Planet-Destination China on-line at www.lonelyplanet.com

INDEX